Unraveling the Illusions

Why You Shouldn't Trust Your Own Thoughts

Rachel Johnson

Table of Contents:

Chapter 1

Chapter 2

• The Benefits of Humility and Openness

Chapter 1

The Illusions We Live In

As humans, we all have a tendency to believe in certain illusions that shape our perception of reality. Some of these illusions may be harmless, while others can be damaging and prevent us from living our lives to the fullest. Here are some of the most common illusions we live in:

1. The illusion of control

Often, we believe that we have more control over our lives than we actually do. We believe that if we do everything right, we can prevent bad things from happening to us. However, the truth is that life is unpredictable, and there are many things outside of our control. By accepting this illusion, we can learn to let go of unrealistic expectations and focus on what we can control.

2. The illusion of permanence

Another illusion we often fall victim to is the illusion of permanence. We believe that things will stay the same forever, and we resist change when it inevitably occurs. This illusion can lead to complacency and prevent us from taking risks and pursuing our dreams. The truth is that everything is temporary, and embracing change can lead to personal growth and new opportunities.

3. The illusion of superiority

Many of us believe that we are better than others, whether it be due to our race, socioeconomic status, or education level. This illusion can lead to prejudice and discrimination and prevent us from seeing the unique qualities that make each individual valuable. By recognizing that everyone has something to offer, we can begin to appreciate the diversity around us.

4. The illusion of perfection

Lastly, we often believe that we must be perfect in order to be happy and successful. This illusion can lead to anxiety and low self-esteem as we chase an unattainable standard. The truth is that no one is perfect, and accepting our flaws can lead to greater self-awareness and the ability to learn from our mistakes.

In conclusion, humans are prone to living in illusions that shape our perceptions of reality. By recognizing these illusions and striving for a more truthful perspective, we can live more meaningful and fulfilling lives.

The Power of Perception

From Reality to Illusions is a journey that we all take throughout our lives. We begin in a world of concrete experience, where everything we perceive is tangible and real. However, as we grow and develop, we slowly begin to explore the world of the imagination and the mind. We move away from the physical and start to explore the abstract, the intangible, and the fantastical.

This journey is fueled by our curiosity, our desire to explore and understand the world around us. It is also influenced by the societal norms and cultural beliefs that we are exposed to. As we are bombarded with images and messages, our perception of reality is shaped and altered, creating a landscape of illusions that can be difficult to navigate.

One of the most significant illusions that we encounter is

the concept of perfection. From an early age, we are taught that we should strive to be perfect in every way. We are encouraged to look a certain way, behave a certain way, and achieve certain goals. However, these standards of perfection are often impossible to attain, and we find ourselves striving for something that is nothing but an illusion.

Another common illusion is the idea of success. We are told that we must succeed in order to be happy and fulfilled, but what exactly does success mean? Is it a high-paying job, a big house, and a fancy car? Or is it something deeper, more personal, and more profound? Often, we chase a notion of success that is not aligned with our true values and desires, and we end up feeling unfulfilled and disillusioned.

Finally, our relationship with technology and social media can create a realm of illusion that feels very real. Through carefully curated images and lifestyles, we present a version of ourselves to the world that is not always authentic. This can lead to a distorted sense of reality, where we compare ourselves to others and feel inadequate, even though the image we're comparing ourselves to is not real.

The journey from reality to illusions is an ongoing process, a path that we navigate throughout our lives. However, by staying true to our values, embracing our imperfections, and being honest with ourselves and others, we can find our way back to a more authentic and meaningful reality.

From Reality to Illusions

From Reality to Illusions is a journey that we all take

throughout our lives. We begin in a world of concrete experience, where everything we perceive is tangible and real. However, as we grow and develop, we slowly begin to explore the world of the imagination and the mind. We move away from the physical and start to explore the abstract, the intangible, and the fantastical.

This journey is fueled by our curiosity, our desire to explore and understand the world around us. It is also influenced by the societal norms and cultural beliefs that we are exposed to. As we are bombarded with images and messages, our perception of reality is shaped and altered, creating a landscape of illusions that can be difficult to navigate.

One of the most significant illusions that we encounter is the concept of perfection. From an early age, we are taught that we should strive to be perfect in every way. We are encouraged to look a certain way, behave a certain way, and achieve certain goals. However, these standards of perfection are often impossible to attain, and we find ourselves striving for something that is nothing but an illusion.

Another common illusion is the idea of success. We are told that we must succeed in order to be happy and fulfilled, but what exactly does success mean? Is it a high-paying job, a big house, and a fancy car? Or is it something deeper, more personal, and more profound? Often, we chase a notion of success that is not aligned with our true values and desires, and we end up feeling unfulfilled and disillusioned.

Finally, our relationship with technology and social media can create a realm of illusion that feels very real. Through carefully curated images and lifestyles, we present a version of ourselves to the world that is not always authentic. This can lead to a distorted sense of reality, where we compare ourselves to others and feel inadequate, even though the image we're comparing ourselves to is not real.

The journey from reality to illusions is an ongoing process, a path that we navigate throughout our lives. However, by staying true to our values, embracing our imperfections, and being honest with ourselves and others, we can find our way back to a more authentic and meaningful reality.

Why You Shouldn't Trust Your Own Thoughts

As human beings, we tend to believe that our thoughts are reliable and trustworthy. After all, we have been using our brains to think and make decisions since we were born. However, the truth is that our own thoughts can often be misleading and biased.

There are many reasons why you shouldn't trust your own thoughts. Firstly, our thoughts are influenced by our emotions. When we are feeling sad, anxious, or angry, our thoughts tend to be negative and distorted. We may jump to conclusions, make assumptions, or focus only on the negative aspects of a situation. This can lead us to make irrational decisions and judgments that we may regret later.

Secondly, our thoughts can be influenced by our past experiences and beliefs. We tend to filter information that fits into our pre-existing beliefs and ignore information that contradicts them. This can create confirmation bias and prevent us from seeing the full picture. We may also generalize based on past experiences, which can limit our ability to consider different perspectives.

Thirdly, our thoughts can be influenced by external factors such as the media, advertisements, and social norms. We may unknowingly adopt beliefs and opinions that are not our own but are instead influenced by the messages we receive from the outside world. This can lead to a lack of critical thinking and a failure to question our own beliefs.

In addition to these factors, our thoughts can also be influenced by cognitive biases such as the availability heuristic, where we judge the likelihood of events based on how easily we can recall them, or the self-serving bias, where we attribute our successes to our abilities but blame our failures on external factors.

In conclusion, it's essential to be aware of these biases and limitations when it comes to our own thoughts. While our thoughts can be valuable and insightful, they can also be misleading and unreliable. It's important to approach our thoughts with a critical eye and be open to considering different perspectives. By doing so, we can make better decisions and avoid the pitfalls of our own biased thinking.

Chapter 2

The Illusion of Memory

Memory is a remarkable function of the human brain. It allows us to relive pleasant moments, learn from mistakes, and connect with our past. However, memory is not a flawless process, as it is susceptible to numerous distortions and illusions. At times, we may believe that our memories are accurate, when in fact, they are merely illusions.

One of the most common illusions of memory is the misattribution of information.

This occurs when our brain confuses the source of the information we have stored. For instance, we may believe that a memory is our own, when in reality, it was something we heard from someone else.

Another illusion of memory is the false memory effect. In this case, people can vividly recall an event that never happened. Several factors can contribute to creating false memories, including post-event information, suggestive questioning, and social conformity.

The reconstructive nature of memory is another factor that contributes to illusions. Our memory is not like a video recorder, which stores events verbatim. Instead, we reconstruct our memories using a combination of factual information, personal bias, and imagination. As a result, we may remember events differently from how they actually occurred.

Moreover, memories are susceptible to fading and becoming distorted over time. People may remember events differently as time passes, and memories can change drastically over several years. This is especially true for traumatic experiences, which can cause inaccurate recollections of the event.

In conclusion, the illusion of memory is a natural phenomenon that occurs due to the limitations of the human brain. People may experience illusions due to misattribution of information, false memory effect, reconstructive nature, and fading of memories. Understanding these limitations can help us become more aware of our own memories and prevent ourselves from becoming misled by them.

Misremembering Past Events

Misremembering past events is a common phenomenon that occurs when our brains fail to store memories accurately. As an AI language model, I do not have a brain like humans, hence I cannot misremember anything. However, I can explain a few things regarding misremembering past events.

As humans, we tend to recall certain events in our lives that we believe to be accurate, but in reality, they may be distorted or completely fabricated. This can happen due to various reasons, including the passage of time, emotional bias, or external influence.

For example, a person who was involved in a car accident may misremember the events leading up to the accident or may remember them in a different order. They may also remember details that did not happen or fail to recall crucial details. This misremembering can also occur in legal cases, leading to false accusations or wrongful convictions.

Moreover, emotional factors like stress, anxiety, or trauma can lead to misremembering. Traumatic events like abuse or assault can cause individuals to repress memories or recall them inaccurately, leading to difficulties in obtaining justice in such cases.

Another common cause of misremembering past events is misinformation or external influence. This happens when individuals are exposed to misleading or false information that may alter their memory of past events. This can be seen in social media, where false news or rumors can spread quickly, leading people to believe in things that did not happen or interpret events differently.

In conclusion, misremembering past events is a common occurrence for humans, and it can lead to many problems in legal cases or personal lives. As an AI language model, I do not remember anything, but I am capable of providing guidance on how to deal with misremembering and ways to avoid it. It is advisable to record essential events as they happen, avoid external influence or misinformation, seek professional help in case of traumatic events, and verify information before believing it.

Memory Reconstruction

Memory reconstruction is the process by which our brain recreates a memory from past experiences. Memories are not fixed structures but rather are dynamic and plastic, and subject to modification each time we revisit them. The process of memory reconstruction occurs when we retrieve a specific memory, and then the brain modifies and rewrites the original memory by incorporating new information or changing existing information.

Memory reconstruction is essential for our mental health and wellbeing as it allows us to make sense of our lives, learn from our mistakes, and build new and better memories. However, this process is not always entirely accurate or reliable, and it can lead to distortions, inaccuracies, and false memories.

One of the most common ways that memory reconstruction occurs is through the influence of external factors such as suggestion, leading questions, or influence from other people. For example, if we are told details that did not happen during an event before we retrieve the memory, the brain may incorporate those details into the memory as if they did happen, leading to a false memory.

Memory reconstruction is also happening all the time in our everyday lives, as the brain continually updates and modifies our memories. This can be seen as we grow older, and our memories of childhood become fuzzier and less vivid, as information from later in life replaces the previous recollections.

In conclusion, memory reconstruction is a fundamental process of the brain that allows us to create and modify memories over time. Understanding this process can help us be more aware and critical of our memories, and also help us recognize when our recollections may be unreliable or distorted.

False Memories

False memories are recollections of events or experiences that did not actually occur. These memories can be vivid and convincing, making the individual believe that they truly happened.

There are various reasons why false memories can occur. One explanation is that the brain sometimes fills in missing gaps or details in a memory, causing it to become altered or distorted. Additionally, external factors such as suggestion or leading questions can also influence a person's memory and lead them to remember things that did not actually happen.

False memories can have significant consequences, particularly in the legal system.

Eyewitnesses, for example, may provide testimony that is based on false memories, leading to wrongful convictions or acquittals. In therapy, false memories can also be created through suggestion or leading questions, potentially causing harm to the patient and creating further psychological distress.

One example of false memories is the phenomenon of recovered memories. These are memories of traumatic events that were allegedly repressed by the individual, only to resurface later in life through therapy or other means.

However, the validity of recovered memories is highly controversial, with some researchers questioning whether they are real memories or simply the result of suggestion.

In conclusion, false memories are a complex and fascinating area of study in psychology. While they can have serious implications, it is important to understand the various factors that can contribute to their formation and to be cautious when interpreting memories as absolute truth.

Chapter 3

The Illusion of Attention

The human mind is complex and capable of processing a tremendous amount of information. However, our attention is limited to only a few things at any given moment. This limitation of our attention can often lead to an illusion that we are paying attention to something when, in reality, we are not.

The illusion of attention can arise in situations where we believe we are fully engaged in a task or activity, but our mind is wandering or distracted. For example, we may be driving on the highway and believe we are paying attention to the road, but our mind may be preoccupied with other thoughts, making it a dangerous situation. Similarly, during a conversation, we may feign interest or nod our heads in agreement, but our mind may be wandering, causing us to miss critical information.

The illusion of attention is made even worse by the digital age we live in today. With multiple gadgets and notifications vying for our attention simultaneously, our ability to focus becomes even more limited. These distractions can often lead to an illusion of attention where we think we are fully engaged in a task, but we are merely skimming the surface, missing vital information or making mistakes.

To avoid the illusion of attention, it is crucial to practice mindfulness and stay focused on the present moment. By staying present, we can train our minds to block out distractions and improve our ability to stay focused. We can also limit our digital interactions to reduce distractions, prioritize our tasks to focus on the important ones first, and actively listen and engage in conversations to avoid missing critical information.

In conclusion, the illusion of attention can be dangerous as it leads us to believe that we are fully engaged, when in reality, our minds are wandering or distracted. We need to practice mindfulness, stay present, and limit our digital distractions to stay focused and avoid missing critical information. By doing so, we can stay safe, productive and efficient in our daily lives.

Multitasking

Multitasking means performing multiple tasks at the same time. It's a skill that many of us boast about having, but is it really that beneficial? While multitasking may appear to improve productivity, it is, in reality, a mere illusion.

When we try to do more than one task simultaneously, we are merely dividing our attention amongst those tasks. As a result, none of the tasks are performed optimally. In fact, multitasking can often be counterproductive and can lead to increased errors, poor quality work, and a longer time to complete the task.

Multitasking is a hindrance to creativity and innovation. When we divide our focus among several tasks, we cut ourselves off from the opportunity to practice deep and focused thinking. We are unable to give our best to any of the tasks, and hence the outcome suffers.

Multitasking can also cause increased stress and anxiety, as we try to juggle many tasks while feeling overwhelmed and under pressure. This can have a negative impact on our mental health and wellbeing, and also affect our ability to make decisions and communicate effectively.

The solution to these problems is to learn to prioritize and to focus on one task at a time. Unveiling the illusion of multitasking is essential for our productivity, creativity, and mental health. By focusing on one task at a time, we enable ourselves to give our best and complete the task effectively and efficiently. This does not mean we should not be flexible and adjust to changing demands. However, it is essential to prioritize and focus on what is essential for optimal performance.

In conclusion, multitasking may appear to be a valuable skill, but in reality, it is an illusion that leads to poor quality work, increased stress, and decreased productivity. By focusing on one task at a time, we enable ourselves to do our best work and achieve success in our endeavors. So let's unveil the illusion of multitasking and focus on being effective, successful, and productive in all aspects of life.

Attentional Blink

Attentional blink is a phenomenon that involves the temporary inability to perceive an object or stimuli that appears immediately after a previous one. This phenomenon has been observed in various contexts, including visual perception, auditory perception, and memory retrieval.

In the context of visual perception, attentional blink is often observed when individuals are shown a rapid, sequential stream of visual stimuli. When individuals are asked to report on two targets that appear within this stream, their ability to identify the second target is often impaired if it occurs within a certain time frame after the first target. This is known as the attentional blink.

One interesting application of attentional blink is in the study of illusions. Illusions are visual experiences that differ from reality and are created by the way our brain processes information. By studying attentional blink, it is possible to better understand why certain illusions work.

For example, the famous Rabbit-Duck illusion is a classic example of how attentional blink affects perception. In this illusion, a drawing of a rabbit can be seen as a duck depending on the viewer's focus. When the viewer focuses on the rabbit's ears, they perceive the rabbit, but when they focus on the bill, they perceive the duck.

The attentional blink explains why some people may not see the illusion immediately. If they are primed to see a rabbit, for example, they may have difficulty shifting their attention to the duck until after the blink has passed. Once the second object is identified, their perception may shift, allowing them to see the illusion.

In conclusion, attentional blink can provide insights into how our brain processes visual information and how this

affects our perception of reality.
By studying attentional blink in
the context of illusions, we can
better understand why some
illusions work and how they
can be used to deceive and
manipulate our perception.

Inattentional Blindness

Inattentional blindness is the
phenomenon where people fail
to perceive or notice something
that is clearly in front of them,
simply because their attention
is focused on something else.
This can often lead to illusions
and misperceptions, which can
have a significant impact on our

understanding of the world around us.

One example of inattentional blindness is the famous Gorilla experiment, where participants were asked to count the number of passes made by players in a basketball game. While they were focused on this task, a person in a gorilla suit walked right through the middle of the players, but only around half of the participants noticed the gorilla.

This demonstrates that when our attention is focused on a specific task or goal, we can miss important details in our environment. Inattentional blindness can lead to the creation of illusions, where we perceive something that is not actually there, or fail to perceive something that is.

For example, in the world of magic and illusion, magicians often use inattentional blindness to create illusions that seem impossible. By directing the audience's attention in a specific way, they can create the perception of something happening that isn't actually occurring.

Understanding inattentional blindness is important, as it can have significant real-world consequences. For example, in driving, drivers may fail to see pedestrians or cyclists because they are focused on something else. This can lead to accidents, injuries, and even fatalities.

Overall, inattentional blindness is a fascinating and complex phenomenon that can lead to both illusions and misperceptions. By being aware of it, we can better understand how our focus can impact our perception of the world around us.

Chapter 4

The Illusion of Confidence

Confidence is a quality that is often admired and envied. People who possess confidence are often perceived as successful, powerful, and admired by others. However, it is important to recognize that confidence can be an illusion, and that many people who appear confident on the surface may actually be struggling with insecurity and self-doubt beneath the surface.

The illusion of confidence can be particularly dangerous when it comes to making important decisions. When individuals are overly confident in their abilities or knowledge, they may fail to consider alternative options or perspectives that could lead to a better outcome. This can result in poor decision-making and negative consequences for themselves and those around them.

Many people who appear confident may also be using this persona as a mask to cover up their insecurities and fears. They may feel pressure to project an image of confidence in order to be successful or to fit in with a certain social group. This can lead to a harmful cycle of striving for external validation and feeling increasingly disconnected from their true selves.

It is important to recognize that true confidence comes from a place of self-awareness and self-acceptance. People who are truly confident are not afraid to acknowledge their weaknesses and vulnerabilities, and are willing to work on themselves to grow and improve. They are also able to recognize the strengths and abilities of others and are willing to collaborate and seek support when needed.

In conclusion, the illusion of confidence can be dangerous and misleading. It is important to recognize that true confidence comes from a place of self-awareness and acceptance, and that we should strive to cultivate this type of confidence in ourselves and those around us. By valuing honesty, vulnerability, and growth, we can create a more supportive and connected community that values individuality and collective success.

Overconfidence Bias

The overconfidence bias refers to our tendency to overestimate our abilities or the accuracy of our predictions. This bias can lead us to make decisions based on flawed assumptions, which can result in negative outcomes.

In the context of unveiling illusions, the overconfidence bias can be particularly problematic. When we believe that we have a complete understanding of a situation, we may be less likely to seek out additional information or alternative perspectives. This can lead us to overlook important details or to make

assumptions that are not
supported by evidence.

For example, consider a
situation in which a group of
investors overconfidently
believes that a particular stock
will perform well in the coming
months. They may ignore
warning signs that suggest that
the stock is overvalued or that
the company's financials are
not as healthy as they appear.
This overconfidence can result
in significant losses when the
stock fails to perform as
expected.

Similarly, the overconfidence

bias can lead people to underestimate the complexity of a given issue or to believe that they have all the answers. This can be particularly problematic when dealing with complex social or political issues that require a deep understanding of history, culture, and other factors.

To overcome the overconfidence bias when unveiling illusions, it is important to remain humble and open-minded. This means recognizing that we may not have all the answers and being willing to seek out additional information or alternative perspectives. It also means being willing to admit when we are wrong and adjust our thinking accordingly.

By recognizing and overcoming the overconfidence bias, we can more effectively navigate complex situations and avoid the negative consequences of flawed assumptions and incomplete information.

Dunning-Kruger Effect

The Dunning-Kruger effect is a cognitive bias that denotes the tendency of people to overestimate their competence in a particular domain while underestimating their incompetence. This phenomenon is particularly observed in individuals with low levels of knowledge, skills, and experience, as they are not aware of their limitations and often operate under the illusion of superiority.

The Dunning-Kruger effect is especially evident in fields where individuals may believe they have a high level of competency, such as in politics, economics, or the arts. Individuals may make decisions or arguments based on biased opinions and beliefs, rather than actual knowledge and research.

However, the Dunning-Kruger effect can be overcome through effective education and training. By acquiring new information, individuals can realize their limitations, allowing them to improve their competence in a given field. It is essential to emphasize that admitting one's limitations is a step towards growth and development.

One effective way to unveil illusions created by Dunning-Kruger effect is to encourage free and open dialogue on a particular subject matter. Allowing diverse opinions and feedback can help individuals identify their areas of ignorance and weaknesses, providing an opportunity for learning and growth.

In conclusion, the Dunning-Kruger effect can create illusions that hinder our personal and professional growth. We must recognize our limitations and strive to continue learning and unlearning to overcome the effect. Only then can we achieve true competence and confidence in our abilities.

Illusory Superiority

Illusory superiority refers to the tendency of people to overestimate their abilities and skills compared to others. This misguided perception is often driven by personal biases, cognitive biases, and other psychological factors. In truth, illusory superiority is nothing more than a self-deception or self-delusion that can have significant impacts on our lives.

Unveiling the illusions of illusory superiority requires a degree of introspection and self-awareness. It means being honest with oneself about one's own abilities, strengths, and limitations. This includes recognizing one's own biases and cognitive flaws that may be driving the illusion of superiority.

Once we acknowledge the reality of our abilities, we can take steps to improve ourselves and hone our skills. It requires humility and a willingness to learn from others, recognizing that everyone is capable of learning and improving.

Moreover, it's essential to surround ourselves with others

who challenge us and push us to be our best selves. People who share similar values and aspirations, but who also can offer different perspectives and ideas, can be instrumental in helping us break down our illusions of superiority.

Unveiling the illusions of illusory superiority can be a humbling experience, but it can also be a powerful motivator for growth and development. When we recognize our limitations and weaknesses, we can focus on developing our strengths and improving our weaknesses, leading to a more fulfilling and satisfying life.

Chapter 5

The Illusion of Control

The human mind is a fascinating and complex entity that seeks to make sense of the world around us. We all have a deep-rooted desire for control, to feel like we have some influence over the course of events in our lives. However, this need for control can sometimes lead us into a false sense of security and an illusion of control.

Illusions are a part of human perception, and we create them unconsciously as a way of making sense of the world around us. However, these illusions can make us feel like we have control over the situations we face, when in reality, we have little or no influence over them.

For instance, in our personal lives, we often try to control everything that happens to us, from the people we interact with to the events that occur. But the truth is, life is unpredictable, and many of the things that happen to us are outside of our control. Believing that we can control even the smallest details of our lives can lead us into a false sense of control, making us vulnerable to disappointment and frustration.

Similarly, in the world of business, leaders often hold the illusion that they control everything that happens in their organization. They believe that they can dictate the outcomes of their endeavors and make everything happen according to their plan. This kind of thinking is a recipe for disaster as it sets unrealistic expectations and creates a culture of blame and finger-pointing when things don't turn out as planned.

In conclusion, the illusion of control can be a dangerous mindset to hold as it can blur our ability to make rational decisions and set us up for disappointment. However, by recognizing that we have limited control over the events that happen to us, we can be more open and receptive to unforeseen circumstances, making us more adaptable in a rapidly changing world. So, let us eliminate the illusion of control and embrace the unknown for what it is, a thrilling adventure full of opportunities to learn and grow.

Illusion of Control Bias

The illusion of control bias is a cognitive phenomenon where individuals overestimate their level of control over events and situations that are in reality beyond their control. It is a powerful cognitive illusion that can lead people to believe that they are able to control their environment and outcomes, even when there is no rational basis for this belief.

The illusion of control bias can manifest in many different ways, from the belief that one can influence the outcome of a coin toss, to the belief that one can control the actions of other people. It can also be seen in the way people approach decision making, with individuals often believing that they have more control over the outcome of a situation than they really do.

One of the ways to unveil the illusions of control bias is to first recognize it in oneself. It is important to understand that this cognitive bias can influence one's judgment and decision making, and can lead to poor outcomes if left unchecked. Once the bias has been acknowledged, it is important to cultivate mindfulness and an awareness of one's own limitations.

Another way to unveil the illusion of control bias is to seek out objective information and feedback. This can come in the form of seeking out opinions from trusted sources, conducting research, or simply being open to criticism and feedback. By seeking out objective information, individuals can gain a more accurate understanding of their level of control and influence, which can help to counteract the effects of the illusion of control bias.

Ultimately, the key to overcoming the illusion of control bias is to cultivate a sense of humility and an acceptance of the inherent uncertainty that exists in life. By acknowledging that there are some things that are simply beyond our control, we can approach decision making and problem solving with a more realistic and grounded perspective, which can lead to better outcomes and a more fulfilling life.

Superstitions and Rituals

Superstitions and rituals are often used to unveil the illusions that we may encounter in our daily lives. These illusions are often created by our own beliefs, societal norms, and cultural background. While some illusions may be harmless, some can have harmful effects on our physical and mental health if left unaddressed. Superstitions and rituals can be used as a means of uncovering these illusions and breaking free from their hold on us.

One way superstitions and rituals can help unveil illusions is by bringing our attention to them. By focusing our attention on a particular area, we become more aware of what is happening around us. This can be especially helpful when dealing with negative beliefs or cultural norms that may be impacting our lives in a negative way.

Another way superstitions and rituals can help unveil illusions is by providing a sense of comfort and security. These practices can provide a feeling of control over our lives, which can be especially important during times of uncertainty or stress. They can also help us connect with our spiritual beliefs, which can be a powerful source of strength and healing.

Superstitions and rituals can also help unveil illusions by creating a sense of community.

These practices are often shared by many people, which can create a sense of camaraderie and support. By participating in these traditions, we can feel a sense of belonging and connection to others who share our beliefs and experiences.

Ultimately, superstitions and rituals can be powerful tools for unveiling illusions and finding deeper meaning in our lives. They can help us see beyond the surface and find deeper truths that may have been hidden from us. Whether we are seeking spiritual guidance, emotional healing, or simply a sense of connection to something larger than ourselves, these practices can provide a path forward.

The Paradox of Control

The paradox of control lies in the illusion that we have control over everything in our lives. We have been brought up to believe that if we work hard enough, plan well, and follow a certain set of rules, we can control our destinies. However, the reality is that no matter how much we try to control our lives, there are always unforeseen variables that come into play, and ultimately, we cannot control everything.

This illusion of control can be harmful in our lives as it can lead us to become anxious, stressed, and overwhelmed. It can also lead us to think that we are solely responsible for our successes and failures, which can lead to a lack of empathy for others who may not have had the same opportunities or privileges as us.

Unveiling this illusion of control requires us to recognize the role that chance, luck, and circumstances play in our lives. It requires us to be humble and acknowledge that we are not in control of everything. We need to learn to be comfortable with uncertainty and the unknown, and to be resilient in the face of adversity.

However, this does not mean that we should give up trying to improve our lives or pursue our goals. Rather, we should recognize that the path to success is not always linear and that setbacks and failures are a natural part of the process. We should also be open to seeking help and support from others, as we cannot accomplish everything on our own.

In conclusion, the paradox of control highlights the importance of recognizing the limits of our control and the role that chance and circumstances play in our lives. It requires us to be humble, resilient, and open to seeking help and support from others. By doing so, we can navigate the uncertainties of life and find fulfillment and success in our endeavors.

Chapter 6

The Illusion of Self

As human beings, we tend to create a solid sense of self - a sense of individuality that is unique only to us. However, it is important to note that this sense of self, this illusion that we have built, may not be a true representation of who we truly are. In many ways, the concept of a self is an illusion that we fabricate to make sense of the world around us.

It is this illusion of self that can be both helpful and harmful. On one hand, it allows us to establish a sense of identity, purpose, and direction in life. On the other hand, it can prevent us from seeing the world and others around us as they truly are. We become trapped in our own perceptions, assumptions, and expectations, not realizing that we are limited by our own illusions.

The process of unveiling these illusions can be difficult and uncomfortable. We may resist acknowledging the inconsistencies between our ideal self and our real self. We may also struggle with the idea of letting go of that which we have held onto for so long. However, it is only through this

process of shedding our
illusions that we can truly
connect with ourselves and
with others.

When we break free from the
illusion of self, we begin to see
the world with fresh eyes. We
are able to embrace our flaws
and imperfections and extend
the same compassion to others.
We become more open-minded,
more empathetic, and more
accepting of those around us.

In conclusion, the illusion of self
is a construct that we create in
order to make sense of the
world around us. However, it

can also limit our ability to truly connect with others and prevent us from seeing the truth. By acknowledging and unveiling these illusions, we can break free from their constraints and experience a greater sense of authenticity and connection.

The Self as a Construct

The concept of the self has been a subject of philosophical and psychological study for centuries. As humans, we are innately curious about who we are and what makes us unique.

However, the idea of the self has also been a source of confusion and disorientation, creating illusions that further complicate our understanding of our essence.

It is common for people to identify with various labels or roles, such as their job, relationships, or personal achievements. These labels are often used to define who we are, but they can be limiting and lead to a sense of self that is contrived and superficial. Instead, we should look beyond the labels and examine the self as a construct.

The self as a construct implies that our identity is not fixed or predetermined but rather shaped by our experiences, interactions, and social context. It is an ongoing process of self-discovery and refinement that changes over time. It is essential to understand that the self is not a static concept but rather a dynamic entity that shifts and evolves as we live our lives.

In order to unveil the illusions of the self, it is important to recognize the influence of external factors such as culture, society, and personal experiences on our self-perception. These factors can create biases and limitations that affect our understanding of who we are.

Furthermore, the role of the unconscious mind in shaping our beliefs and behaviors cannot be overlooked. The unconscious mind acts as a filter, shaping our perceptions of reality and influencing our actions without our conscious awareness.

By understanding the self as a construct, we can begin to break down these illusions and gain a deeper understanding of our true identity. We can unlock our full potential and lead a life that is authentic and meaningful.

In conclusion, the self as a construct is an essential concept that helps us navigate the complexities of our identity. By recognizing the illusions created by external factors and the unconscious mind, we can unveil the true essence of our being and live a life that is authentic and fulfilling.

Self-Enhancement Bias

Self-enhancement bias refers to the tendency of individuals to view themselves in a more positive light than others. This bias is often responsible for the illusions we hold about ourselves and our abilities, which can lead to overconfidence and complacency. It is important to unveil these illusions to become more self-aware and improve our performance.

Unveiling these illusions requires an honest assessment of our abilities and shortcomings. We need to be willing to accept feedback from others and challenge our own beliefs. This can be difficult, as it requires us to confront our own biases and question our assumptions.

However, by doing this, we can gain a more accurate understanding of our strengths and weaknesses, and work to improve them. This, in turn, can lead to greater success and personal growth.

Some strategies to help unveil our illusions include journaling, seeking feedback, and practicing self-reflection. By engaging in these activities, we can become more aware of our biases and tendencies, and work to overcome them.

Overall, it is important to recognize the role that self-enhancement bias plays in our perceptions of ourselves and the world around us. By actively overcoming this bias and unveiling our illusions, we can become more self-aware and improve our performance and personal growth.

The Illusion of Free Will

The concept of free will has been hotly debated throughout human history. Some argue that we have complete control over our thoughts and actions, while others believe that our choices are predetermined by factors beyond our control. However, recent studies in the fields of neuroscience and psychology have shed new light on the nature of free will, suggesting that it may be nothing more than an illusion.

The idea that free will is an illusion is based on the fact that our brains make decisions before we are consciously aware of them. In other words, the brain is active in making choices before we even realize we are making them. This suggests that our decisions are influenced by unconscious processes that we have no control over.

Furthermore, our environment and upbringing play a significant role in shaping our choices. Our social, cultural, and economic backgrounds all shape our experiences and shape our beliefs, which in turn influence our decisions. We are also subject to biases and heuristics that impact our decision-making, despite our best intentions.

But perhaps the most convincing argument against free will is the fact that we cannot control our desires and motivations. We may be able to control our actions, but we cannot control what we want or how we feel. Our desires and motivations are often at odds with our conscious intentions, leading to conflicting thoughts and actions.

While the idea that free will is an illusion may be unsettling, it can also be liberating. By acknowledging that our choices are influenced by factors beyond our control, we can focus on changing the conditions that shape our decisions. We can work to create an environment that fosters positive behavior and decisions, rather than relying solely on individual willpower.

In conclusion, the notion of free will may be an illusion, and our choices are influenced by unconscious processes, external factors, and innate desires. Understanding the limits of our control can help us make better decisions, and create a more just and equitable society.

Chapter 7

Moving Beyond the Illusions

Human beings have been mesmerized by illusions for centuries. Illusions are defined as misinterpretations or misrepresentations of reality. They have the ability to captivate our imaginations and make us believe that what we are seeing is real. However, countless individuals are starting to realize that these illusions have been holding them back from experiencing life to the fullest.

Moving beyond illusions is a key factor in elevating our

mindset, unleashing unlimited potential, and unlocking a meaningful existence. The evolution of technology and communication in our modern world has made it easier for people to discover and unveil illusions. For instance, the proliferation of social media platforms, which showcase perfect-looking individuals and picture-perfect lifestyles, has dispelled the myth of the perfect life. Additionally, the study of human psychology has shown that our minds are naturally inclined to believe in illusions due to our past experiences, emotions, and expectations.

By unraveling the illusions that have been controlling our lives, we move closer to an authentic life. We begin to realize that we have the power to control our thoughts and emotions, instead of being influenced by them. We discover that all the anxiety, fear, and stress we experience are the result of illusions that we have been holding onto. Moving beyond the illusions enables us to regain control over our lives, and live with a sense of peace and fulfillment.

Furthermore, moving beyond illusions also allows us to detach ourselves from the superficialities of life. We realize that we have been focusing on material possessions, the validation of others, and the opinions of society instead of our own authentic desires. The ability to detach helps us to live a simpler life of gratitude, appreciate life's small moments, and focus on what truly matters.

In conclusion, moving beyond illusions requires a conscious effort to understand our thought processes, control our emotions, and detach from superficialities. It is a journey of self-discovery, growth, and transformation. It is the path to unlocking our truest and most fulfilling life.

The Value of Awareness

Awareness is a crucial factor in revealing illusions that obscure our view of the world. Illusions are perceptions that are misleading or false, but many people unknowingly accept them as reality. They can be challenging to break through without the power of awareness.

Awareness allows us to access our subconscious thoughts and beliefs, and it helps us critically evaluate our experiences, thoughts, and emotions. By becoming aware of our thought patterns and beliefs, we can challenge them and discard the ones that limit us. With awareness, one can understand the nature of illusions and how they manifest in our lives.

Unknowingly, we create illusions for ourselves about our lives, the people around us, and the world at large. These illusions often reflect our fears, insecurities, and biases, and they can hinder our ability to live a happy and satisfying life. They can manifest in the form of limiting beliefs, negative self-talk, irrational fears, and prejudices. By becoming aware of these illusions, we can work to overcome them and gain a clearer, more accurate view of ourselves and the world.

Awareness also brings a sense of mindfulness and consciousness to our lives. It allows us to focus on the present moment and to observe our thoughts and emotions without judgment. This mindfulness helps us to be more aware of our needs, wants, and feelings, and we can respond to them more effectively. By connecting with our inner selves, we gain a deeper understanding of our

purpose and meaning in life
and are more likely to live
authentically.

In conclusion, the value of
awareness on unveiling the
illusions cannot be overstated.
It enables us to challenge our
beliefs, overcome our biases,
and see the world more
objectively. We are more likely
to gain a sense of mindfulness
and consciousness in our lives
and experience greater
fulfillment and personal growth.
By cultivating awareness, we
can live a more satisfying and
fulfilling life, free from the
illusions that once held us back.

Strategies for Overcoming Illusions

Many people go through life with illusions that prevent them from reaching their full potential. These illusions can be negative beliefs about themselves, misconceptions about the world, or limiting thoughts that restrict their growth. Overcoming these illusions is a critical step to realizing our potential and achieving success. Here are some strategies for unveiling and overcoming illusions:

1. Recognize and name the illusion: The first step in overcoming any illusion is to

become aware of it. Identify what the illusion is and name it. This can help you objectify the illusion and distance yourself from it.

2. Question the illusion: Illusions often arise from faulty thinking or incorrect assumptions. Question the validity of the illusion and try to understand where it came from. This process can help to reveal the underlying beliefs that need to be challenged.

3. Challenge your beliefs: When you identify the underlying beliefs that support the illusion,

examine them carefully. Ask yourself if these beliefs are accurate and helpful or if they are holding you back. Look for evidence that supports or refutes these beliefs.

4. Seek third-party perspectives: Sometimes, it can be challenging to identify and overcome illusions on our own. Seeking input from trusted friends, family members, or colleagues can provide a fresh perspective and challenge our preconceived notions.

5. Practice mindfulness: Cultivating a mindful

awareness of our thoughts, emotions, and surroundings can help us identify when illusions arise. With time and practice, this can help us recognize and overcome harmful illusions.

6. Establish realistic goals: Overcoming illusions can be a challenging process, so it's important to set realistic goals. Break the process down into small steps and celebrate each milestone along the way.

7. Stay curious: The process of overcoming illusions is an ongoing one. Keep an open mind and stay curious about the

world around you. Challenge assumptions and continue to grow and evolve.

In summary, overcoming illusions requires self-awareness, curiosity, and a willingness to challenge our beliefs. With these strategies, we can identify and overcome limiting illusions, allowing us to achieve our full potential and create the life we desire.

The Benefits of Humility and Openness

Humility and openness are two very important traits in the pursuit of unveiling illusions. When one is humble, they are open to the fact that they don't know everything and are willing to learn from others. When one is open, they are willing to listen to different perspectives and ideas, instead of being closed-minded and only seeing things from their own point of view. These two traits are essential in helping to uncover illusions that may be clouding one's judgment and preventing them from seeing things as they truly are.

One of the benefits of humility is that it allows us to be honest with ourselves. When we are humble, we are more likely to admit when we are wrong or when we don't know something. This is important when trying to uncover illusions because it allows us to acknowledge that our current understanding of something may be incorrect. Without this humility, we may be blinded by our own beliefs and unable to see the truth.

Another benefit of openness is that it allows us to consider different viewpoints. When we are open to hearing what others have to say, we are able to take in a wider range of ideas and opinions. This is important when trying to uncover illusions because we may be exposed to ideas that we had never considered before. By being open, we are more likely to discover the truth, even if it requires us to question our own beliefs.

Together, humility and openness make a powerful combination in the pursuit of unveiling illusions. By being humble, we are able to admit when we don't know something and are more willing to learn from others. By being open, we are able to consider different perspectives and ideas. These traits allow us to remove the blinders that can prevent us from seeing things as they truly are. By embracing these traits, we can gain a deeper understanding of the world around us and make better, more informed decisions.